# Are We There Yet?
# ALL About the Planet Venus!

## Space for Kids
## Children's Aeronautics & Space Book

**BABY PROFESSOR**

EDUCATION KIDS

# FACTS ABOUT
# PLANET VENUS

Venus is the
second planet
from the sun
next to Mercury.

There are many volcanoes found in Venus.

Venus is the second brightest object in the sky, next to moon.

Venus has an
atmosphere and
it is made up of
carbon dioxide.

Venus is the hottest planet in the solar system.

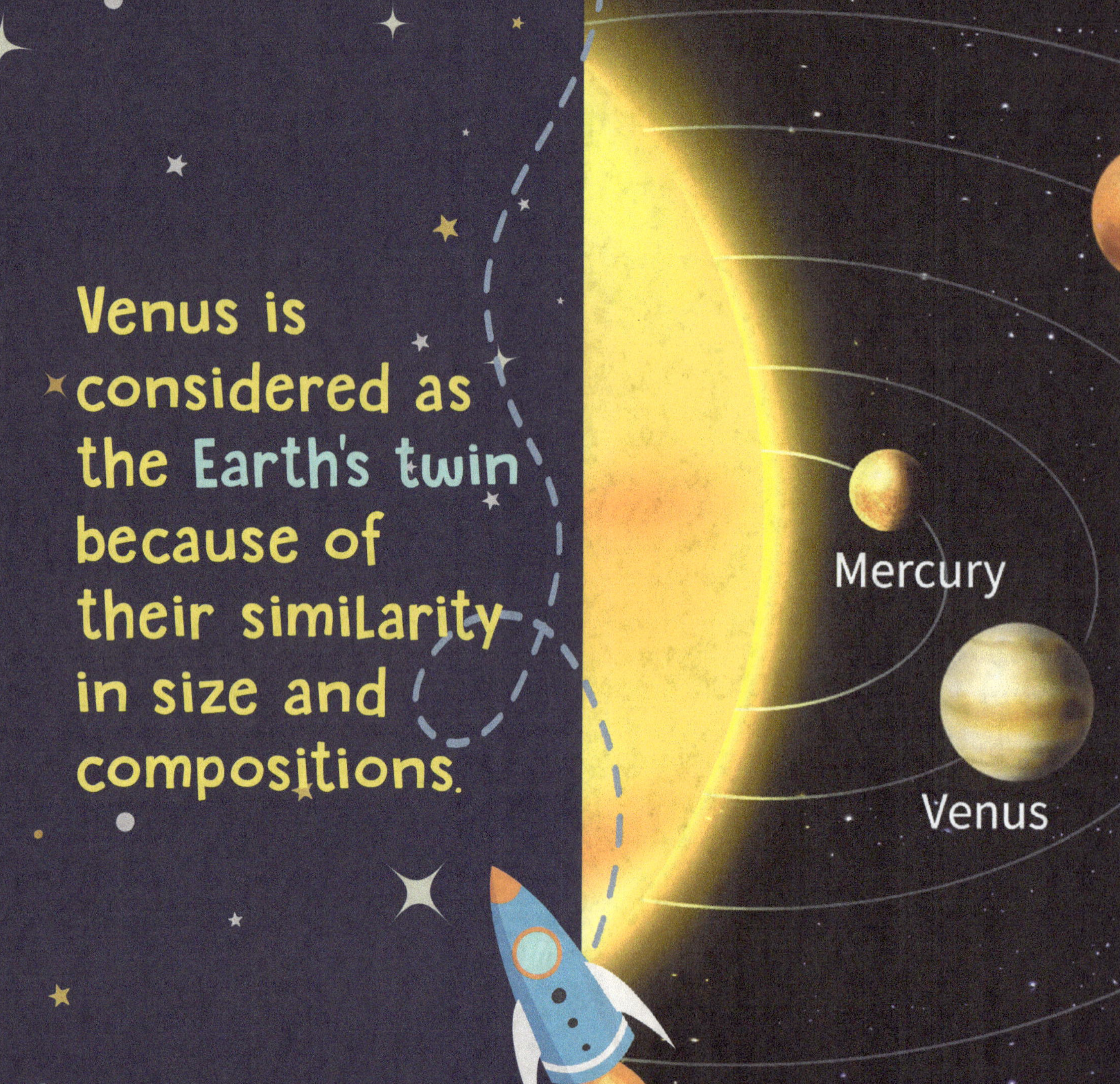


Venus is considered as the Earth's twin because of their similarity in size and compositions.

Mars
Saturn
Pluto
Earth
Jupiter
Neptune
Uranus

There is no
water in Venus.

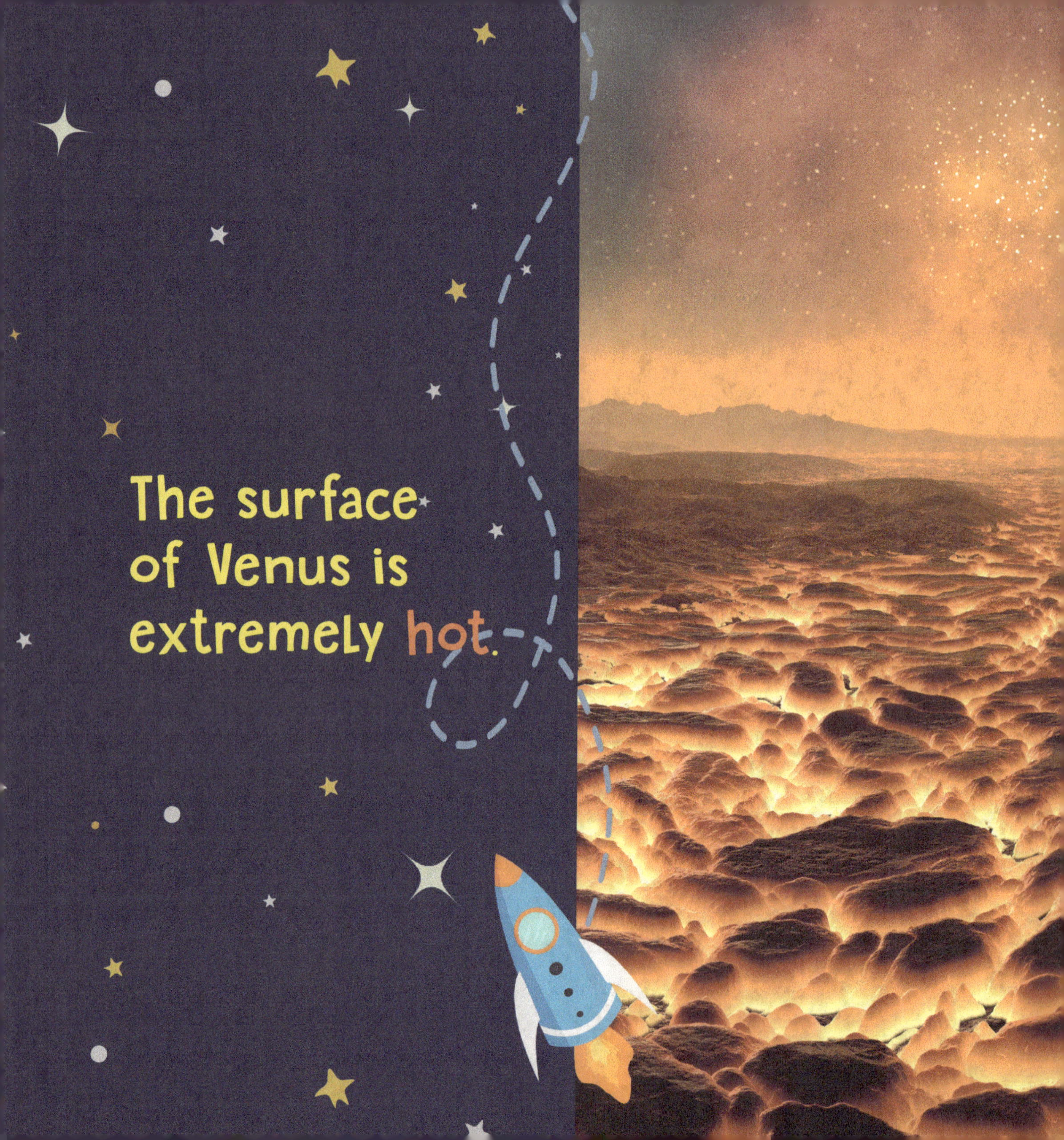
The surface
of Venus is
extremely hot.

Venus is the only planet in the solar sytem that rotates in the opposite direction than most other planets.

The surface of
Venus is full of
crater and very
active volcanoes.

Venus is a windy
planet. It has
an extreme air
pressure just
like the water
pressure of
Earth.

A day in Venus
is Longer than a
year.

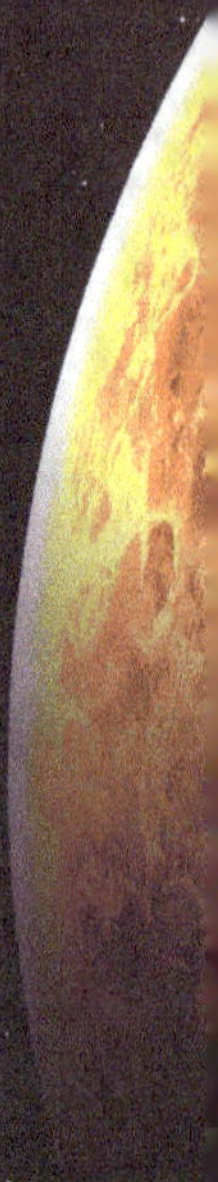

Venus has
gravity similar
to Earth.

The climate
of Venus was
similar to
Earth billion
years ago.

The clouds
in Venus are
so thick. The
temperature of
Venus during
daytime is similar
to night time.

A collision to
an asteroid was
believed to be
the reason for
Venus having
a different
rotation.

Venus is a bit
smaller than
its sister planet
Earth.

Did you learn a lot about Venus? Keep reading! Remember, knowledge is Power!

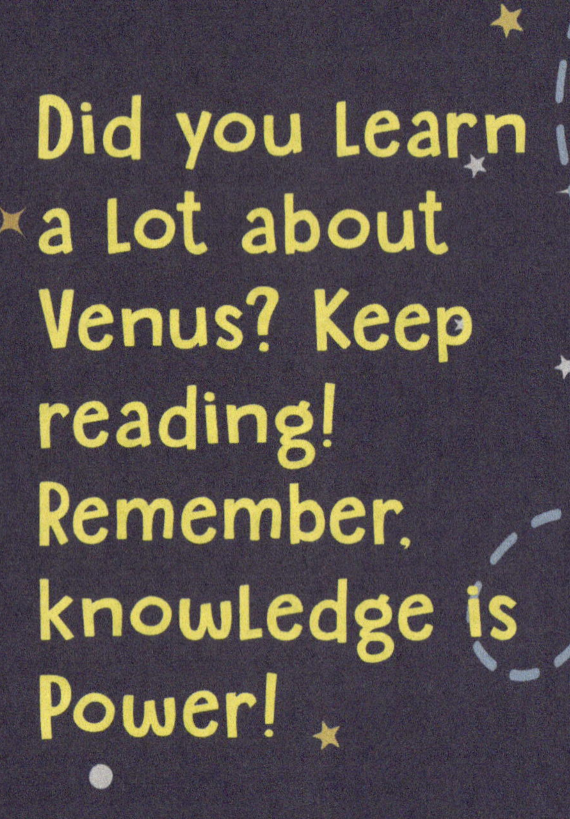

Mars
Saturn
Pluto
Earth
Neptune
Jupiter
Uranus

Visit

BABY PROFESSOR
EDUCATION KIDS

# www.BabyProfessorBooks.com

to download Free Baby Professor eBooks
and view our catalog of new and exciting
Children's Books